REFLECTIONS

Marjorie A. Gillis

FOREWORD

Writing has been something I've enjoyed doing most of my 83 years and putting thoughts to meter and rhyme "just happens!" Writing a poem for a special occasion in someone's life was gratifying to me, and it almost became funny when someone would say, "You should write a book!"

On a recent visit for my birthday, my daughter Joyce began helping me to collect those poems that we could easily find (for they are scribbled in every notebook and folder, many of them unfinished), and she encouraged me to "think about putting them into book form."

More recently, my daughter Jan found a way to publish online and has been instrumental in getting this project going. When it came to illustrating the book, my son Jay and his wife Pamela agreed to use some of their beautiful photography and choreographed the pages. I'm proud of what each of them has done, and now you see the finished product--a collaboration of love!

DEDICATION

*This book is dedicated to my husband Claude
(Gil), to my children and my friends,
with love and thanks for all the times through
the years they encouraged me to write,
and to my Father in Heaven, who inspired me
to do so.*

Table of Contents

Inspirational	1
Poems for Family	31
Poems for Friends	55
Special Occasions	69
Card Sentiments	77
Whimsical	95

Inspirational

HEAVEN

We really don't know what Heaven will be like.
But we do know that it will be grand;
For just living here on this earth is a clue
When we see the great works of God's hand:
In the sunset that clean takes our breath full away;
In the songs that bring tears to our eyes;
In the awe that the birth of a new baby brings;
In the great majesty of the skies!

When we view all the wonders that bless our lives here,
(And we know these are just for a time);
When we read of His promise to ready a home
Far beyond what we see in our minds;
How our life here on earth is compared to a seed
That will blossom in the garden above;
Then the best part will be when we meet Jesus there
And we'll praise Him forever in love!

MY DAILY PRAYERS

I pray every day for my family and friends;
For those that are ailing, that their bodies will mend;
For the elderly and newborns—the caring they need;
For those who've lost loved ones and are feeling bereaved;
For those newly married with adjustments to make;
For all those new Christians, the baby steps they must take;
For people we meet every week while we're shopping;
With thanks for those friends who pray for us without stopping.
For His church, and this country—how we need Him right now
To turn things around—would He please show us how.

I know that the Lord knows before I do pray,
With no doubts that He'll answer in His own time and way.

HE'S WAITING FOR YOU

Come, you who are weary with burden so heavy,
The Lord is just waiting to share it with you.
The yoke that He offers will sit on you lightly,
And shoulder to shoulder He'll walk close to you.

Come quickly, don't tarry! Your sorrows He'll soften;
Your most secret thoughts He will understand, too.
Your sins He'll forgive if you truly are sorry—
(What friend in this life makes this promise to you?)

Yes, come with your toubles and tell them to Jesus;
Give Him your love and obedience, too.
Soon you will find that your burden has vanished.
Yes, Jesus is waiting—He's waiting for you!

HELP ME BE A BETTER ME

God sees the things that I have done—
The overt act, the hidden one;
He knows the things that I have thought,
The inner battles being fought;
He knows the masks that play a part,
Hiding feelings in my heart;
Yet still He loves me tenderly—
"Lord, help me be a better me!"

OUR GREAT AND WONDERFUL GOD

Who is this God called "The Great I Am"
Who long before time developed a plan
To create a great universe of unlimited span
With a finely built planet upon which He placed man?

Who is this God who is 3 but just One:
God, the Father; the Spirit; and Jesus, the Son?
Although each one plays a separate part,
They're truly connected in purpose and heart.

Who is the Father, what part does He play?
He watches His children and hears when they pray;
He oversees all that His world must endure
From Satan's great wiles aimed to keep it impure.

Who is the Spirit, and what does He do?
If you are the Lord's, then He's living in you--
He helps you and guides you, provides you a sword
To fight your life battles—it's found in His Word.

And who is this Jesus, what is His role?
He came for the purpose of saving your soul.
He pleads to the Father, forgiveness His goal--
The blood of His sacrifice making you whole.

So simple, yet complex; so mighty and true;
How The God of the Universe listens to you,
And comforts and loves you in spite of your sin—
The promise of Heaven, may we hear "Enter in!"

FELLOWSHIP

When you consider the word "fellowship"
of what do you think?
A fellowship could be a covered-dish dinner
with iced tea to drink.
We might consider communion as a fellowship
with those of like kind;
Or perhaps it's a good friend which whom you
can share the thoughts of your mind.

Yes, fellowship can be all those things but it
encompasses so much more:
It's really a "relationship with God" as its
purpose and core.
It's having communion with Him in everything
that we do—
Living each day with His blessings and His
presence in view.

How awesome to know that our Father God
wants us to share
Those blessings He gives us by word, deed
and prayer.
With His Spirit to guide us in a "partnership
of love and accord"
We then understand what it means to have
"fellowship with the Lord."

SUMMER DAWN

The day dawns brightly o'er
the brow;
The leaves are brushed with
silv'ry sheen;
All earth is hushed save
birdsong now
And all the grass is lush
and green.

No artist's brush nor
poet's pen
Could capture such a scene
so rare;
The Master's touch is in
the glen,
For God is there—yes, God
is there!

HOW MANY TIMES?

How many times have you blessed me, Lord,
While I was unaware?
How many times forgiven me
In answer to my prayer?
How many times have you lifted me
To help me through the day;
And how many times have you blocked my path
From taking the wrong way?

Oh, Lord, You know how many times—
Too numerous to count;
Yet in Your love, through Jesus' blood,
You've cancelled my account!
How much I owe, You only know;
Grant the rest of this life may be
Lived close to You so that my thanks may go
On neverendingly.

HOPE

What did you hope for when you were young--
Things you might want right away;
A doll, or some skates or a trip to the park—
'Twas hard to wait more than a day!

A little bit older and then it was school--
Seemed like it never would come;
But before you could blink it was all in the past
And that part of your life was all done!

Then it's onto the workplace to work out your plan
For the dreams that you hoped would come true;
Searching meanwhile for the love of your life--
That one who'd be perfect for you!

And then it was family and all that entails—
You wanted the best for each one;
Then came the grandchildren and even the "grands,"
And another life-cycle's begun.

Now, most of those wishes are all in the past,
(And some of them even came true);
But our hope will be realized through The One Whom We Love,
And will last an eternity through!

MY MOTHER'S GARDEN

My mother has a garden
   That's lovely to behold.
It is the labor of her love
   And hands in hours untold.
She softens all the earth around
   Before she plants her seeds;
Then waters, feeds, and sprays and tills,
   And plucks out all the weeds.
Though all these things alone were done,
   Her labor be in vain,
For God still holds the keys to life
   And sends the sun and rain.
So when we walk in her garden,
   Oh, what loveliness is there;
But only God and mother know
   The secrets that they share!

Life is like that garden
   Wherein we plant our seeds.
Although we want just flowers to grow,
   Among them grow the weeds.
So we must plant and prune until
   The good and best prevail,
And pluck away the seeds of sin—
   Whatever that entail.
But though we worked on endlessly,
   Our labor be in vain
For God still holds the keys of life
   (In Him we are sustained).
So when others view our garden,
   May only beauty show,
And all the toil a secret be
   That only God may know.

LOVE LETTERS

Did you ever get a letter that meant so much to you
That you kept it safe for many years and read it through and through?
You felt the love within those words in every single line
And know the one who wrote it had a "special you" in mind.
Perhaps you felt unworthy at the time when you first read
And thought they might be thinking of another one instead;
But through the years those words took hold and changed your life somehow,
And you hope the one who wrote it would be proud to see you now.

*Did you ever think the Bible is God's letter sent
to you?
Have you kept it close for many years and read it
through and through?
Have you felt the love within His words in every
single line,
And know the One Who wrote it had a "special
you" in mind?
Perhaps you felt unworthy at the time when you
first read
And thought He might be thinking of another
one instead;
But through the years His words took hold and
changed your life somehow
And you pray the One Who wrote it would be proud
to see you now.*

THANKFUL FOR THE MEMORIES

We're thankful for the memories of people in our past;
The ones who loved and nurtured us, and held us close and fast;
Who showed us how to laugh and play and taught us right from wrong;
And also "Jesus Loves Me" was more than just a song.

We're thankful for the teachers who were zealous in their task
Of helping find our talents and the questions we should ask;
Of pointing us the way to find some purpose in our goals,
For through their dedication, they were nurturing our souls.

We're thankful for the friends who walked beside us all the way,
And even some who blessed our lives for just a little day;
Especially those who held our hands when we have felt depressed,
Or praised our efforts even when we failed to do our best.

We're thankful for the mates who blessed our lives and others, too;
And for the children-- we have tried to give them back to You.
We're thankful for the things we've done and places we have been
Enjoying all the beauty you provide this side of Heav'n.

Yes, we're thankful for our memories, even those we can't recall,
For although we do forget, we are made up of them all.
So, thank you, Lord, for memories that shaped the essence of our past,
And we pray those in our future will be blessings that will last.

MY MORNING PRAYER

Lord, help me live this day
As though it were my last—
Not longing for the morrow,
Nor dreaming of the past;
But let this day an island be,
Though it shores be wracked by stormy sea;
Let Thy hand be there to comfort me
And keep calm in my soul.

MY WAKING-UP PRAYER

Lord, thank you for my nice warm bed
And the roof above my head;
For the love beside me sleeping
And the sun through shades a-creeping.

Thank you for this brand-new day
And whatever comes my way;
May everything I say and do
Become my sacrifice to You.

OUR UNCHANGING GOD

We never know what life will bring:
The happiness; the fearful thing;
The poverty or yet the wealth;
The sturdy frame; the loss of health.

In faith we live from day to day
Doing our best to follow His Way,
Not to be shaken by the blows
That plunge us from our highs to lows.

Through all, we know that He is there,
The One Who keeps us in His care,
Who teaches us that life is worth
Every challenge here on earth.

So mountain high or valley low,
Knowing He's with us wherever we go.
In our changing world, we must endure,
Knowing whatever comes, His promise is sure.

PRAYER

When weariness comes from the world and its pace,
He leads me to a deserted place
Where all is still.

He listens with interest to what I say
And channels my thoughts to the better way
Which is His Will.

He forgives the sins from which I've turned;
And in the knowledge that He's concerned,
All cares grow dim.

The effects of His presence refreshing my soul,
It's back to the world, once again whole,
To live for Him.

PEACE OF MIND

Whenever I am worried and my heart is full of care,
You tell me, "Do not be anxious for I know the load you bear."
That encouraging piece of Your mind brings sweet peace to my mind
And I know that you are there.

Whenever I'm feeling lonely and my friends don't understand,
You say, "I am with you always and closer than any man."
That comforting piece of Your mind brings such peace to my mind
That I feel You are holding my hand.

When anger boils inside me and injustice seems to reign,
The thought of the cross and the unjustness You faced helps to relieve the pain.
That great piece of Your mind brings humbling peace to my mind,
And I begin to think clearly again.

When someone asks forgiveness but the hurt will not let go,
"Forgive as you have been forgiven" are the words You want me to know.
That amazing piece of Your mind brings awesome peace to my mind
And my heart is made light in its glow.

And whenever I am concerned about the state of my soul,
You remind me I've been "washed in the blood and made whole."
That glorious piece of Your mind brings saving peace to my mind—
for eternity with You is my goal!

SING, PRAY AND WORK

Sing when you're happy, sing when you're sad,
Sing while you're washing the dishes; ☺
Sing with your heart full of love for His grace;
Ever aware what His wish is.

Pray when you're thankful, pray when there's need,
Pray for the Spirit to guide you;
Pray when you're lonely, pray when you hurt,
And pray that He'll stay close beside you.

Work what's before you, what needs to be done,
Aware of the needs close around you;
Work with a will all that God sends your way,
Bearing fruit in the lives that surround you.

Singing and praying and working for Him--
What happier life is there given?
Though Satan will threaten to undermine all,
God's promised there's singing in Heaven!

SPRING CLEANING

Throw open the doors of your heart;
Unlock the shutters of your mind;
Let the gentle breeze of fresh ideas
Every dusty corner find.

Inhale deeply the Breath of Life;
Wash every dark spot and stain;
Polish every facet of your soul—
Let no untouched spot remain.

Discard thoughts impure or unkind
And replace with a bouquet of prayer.
Determine you'll e'er keep your temple
    this clean
For the Spirit of God dwelling there!

THE ANSWER

There have been times when most of us have felt so much alone;
Perhaps we've lost a loved one, or moved to a new home.
Could be our name has been besmirched with no recourse to take;
Our feelings hurt by one we love which causes much heartache.
When no one seems to understand the pain we're going through,
We sit alone and bow our heads and shed a tear or two.
"Can no one help me overcome this grief and hopelessness?"
Of course we know the answer! Our Savior answers "Yes!"

"I came from Heaven to understand what life on earth can bring;
"To show you how to rise above your hurt and suffering.
"I offer you my comfort, for I can share your pain,
"And give you grace to face your cares, to live fully free again!"
So when we're feeling lonely, we can know He understands;
He will help us lay aside our griefs if we put them in His hands.
Our hearts will then be lightened as we reach for happiness;
For in Jesus Christ, our Savior, His answer's always "Yes!"

THE BLESSINGS OF SONG

A little bird sat in our tree yesterday;
He opened his throat and he warbled away.
This short little concert was such a surprise,
And the joy of his song brought tears to my eyes!

I thought, "What a blessing God planned for
                mankind—
The beauty of melody there in His mind;
Even before the foundation of earth
He knew what the value of music was worth!"

And our little bird had his own song to sing
Of a lovely warm day and the portent of Spring.
He sang as the Lord gave him talent to do
Just as He gave some to me and to you.

And He tells us to sing with our heart and our soul
To praise Him and thank Him our primary goal--
A marvelous way for His story to tell,
To teach and encourage each other as well.

So now when I'm naming my blessings to count,
There's another one added to that endless amount.
That little bird sang--what we've known all along:
The music of life is eternity's song!

THE CHRISTIAN'S GOAL

A God to glorify each day;
A Savior' steps to lead the way;
A life to live that's free from sin;
A soul to seek—perhaps to win;
A healthy mind and body, too;
Love to give; work to do;
The world, to guard against it's snare;
Temptation to resist with prayer;
Eternity to think upon;
Heaven to seek in the life beyond.

If all these seeds in life are sown,
Then death will be "just going home!"

THE SONGS WE SING

The songs we sing—they bring us joy
And sometimes cause us tears;
The words and melodies so joined
Bring mem'ries through the years.

The songs we sing—they help to teach
Ourselves and others, too,
Reminding us how we should live
And what we're called to do.

The songs we sing—they help us praise
Our God in Heaven above
With thoughts our feeble minds can't raise
In answer to His love.

The songs we sing—oh, let them be
The worship of our soul
To Jesus Christ, our Savior, friend,
For He can make us whole.

So lift your head, your heart, your soul
And let our voices bring
All glory to the God we love
By these—the songs we sing!

THE HEART OF THE MATTER

I saw the inside of Claude's heart yesterday.
A machine showed this mass of flesh pumping away.
It squeezed and retracted, fascinating to see—
In some ways repulsive and unbelievable to me.
To think that the Lord had designed such a plan
To keep the blood flowing in the body of man—
The blood that brings living to each vital part,
Recycled and purified, emanates from the heart.

We can all see inside of God's heart every day.
The Word shows the proof of his love through The Way—
The marvelous working of all He had planned
To offer salvation and forgiveness to man.
That plan which was started before time was begun
Was completed and sealed by the blood of His Son.
That blood brings forgiveness to each vital part,
Offers life everlasting and emanates from His heart!

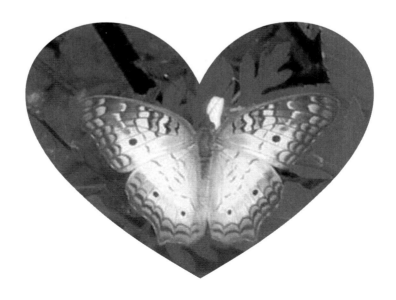

THE KEYS TO HAPPINESS
a poem inspired by my mother

Here are the keys to a rich, happy life:
Enjoy what you have while you have it;
For nothing will last,
Even time will soon pass—
There is aught you can do that will save it!

And all that you do, you can do with a will,
For each moment's a gift, don't refuse it;
So whatever the day,
Give your best all the way--
There is happiness there if you choose it!

But God holds the keys to the happiest life
When the gifts that He gives are not wasted.
When you show that you care,
When you love and you share,
Then a small bit of Heaven is tasted!

THOUGHTS DURING COMMUNION

My sins have pierced Thy blessed feet
And nailed Thy hands upon the tree;
That crown of thorns upon Thy head
Was worn for me...for me...for me!

O suffering, painful, shameful scene,
My tears can dim to none degree!
What selflessness! What love was shown!
O Lord, for me...for me...for me!

What answer? What response to this?
Is there nothing I can do?
The answer from above is clear:
Yes, I must live for You...for You!

WHAT IS GOD LIKE?

*How can we really know This One whom we
    have never seen with our eyes,
Whom we have never touched with our hands to
    determine His form or His size;
And we have never heard His voice to guide our
    lives through the years,
Nor smelled His presence, nor heard Him laugh,
    nor tasted of His tears?*

*Our earthly beings, so finite, can't seem to grasp
    the greatness of His power and might;
Yet we can catch a glimpse of all He is and does,
    by the gift of faith and not by sight.
This mighty God who made the world is Father
    of all, our perfect and sure guide;
We can feel His presence and know He hears when
    we earnestly pray for His Spirit to abide.*

This almighty, all-wise Father of all, Who is every-
*   where and knows our every need;*
Is the righteous One who will judge us in the end
*   by our every word and deed.*
Tempered by His love, He will forgive our sins
*   through Him Who paid our debt in full*
If we have surrendered our lives in obedience
*   and submission to His rule.*

So, can we know what God is like? Oh, yes!
*   His Son came to show man His Way;*
And the Word was inspired to be written for us
*   who were born in a later day.*
Our all-powerful, all-knowing, ever-present God
*   may be awesome and so far above,*
But He calls us to Him and He opens His arms
*   and He wraps all His children in love!*

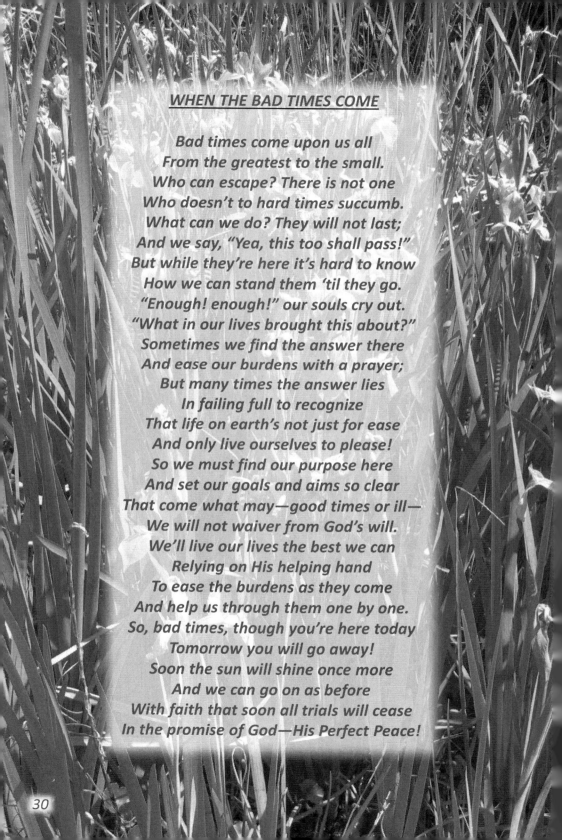

WHEN THE BAD TIMES COME

Bad times come upon us all
From the greatest to the small.
Who can escape? There is not one
Who doesn't to hard times succumb.
What can we do? They will not last;
And we say, "Yea, this too shall pass!"
But while they're here it's hard to know
How we can stand them 'til they go.
"Enough! enough!" our souls cry out.
"What in our lives brought this about?"
Sometimes we find the answer there
And ease our burdens with a prayer;
But many times the answer lies
In failing full to recognize
That life on earth's not just for ease
And only live ourselves to please!
So we must find our purpose here
And set our goals and aims so clear
That come what may—good times or ill—
We will not waiver from God's will.
We'll live our lives the best we can
Relying on His helping hand
To ease the burdens as they come
And help us through them one by one.
So, bad times, though you're here today
Tomorrow you will go away!
Soon the sun will shine once more
And we can go on as before
With faith that soon all trials will cease
In the promise of God—His Perfect Peace!

Poems for Family

TO GIL ON OUR 40TH

Forty years and can it be
That you are still in love with me?
The times we've shared, both good and bad--
The ones that made us happy, sad--
Are wov'n together to make "One Life"
That we have shared as man and wife.
Forty years and it is true
That I am still in love with you!

TO GIL ON OUR 45TH

The Lord has blessed us many years.
He's seen us through both joy and tears;
And you've been there to hold my hand,
And always tried to understand;
No matter where our lives have led
With words both spoken and unsaid,
We've walked together hand in glove,
And I'm so thankful for my friend, my love!

TO GIL ON HIS 85TH BIRTHDAY

When you were born on that hot July morn
Who knew what the future would hold:
From runner to milkman to preacher, for some
Of the many "hats" no one foretold.

Your names have been legion from Junior to Gil
To Brother Gillis and now it's just Claude,
Except for the grandkids who call you Granddaddy
With "Grumpy" thrown in! (You're a fraud)!

From husband to father to grampa and "great"—
The pleasure of living so long
With a family who loves you and wants just the best
For the rest of your life. (Can't go wrong)!

It's not always been easy but God paved the way
For the love with which we've been blessed!
Now enjoy this next year while we watch and we pray
And we see what He does with the rest!

HAPPY ANNIVERSARY

Through the good times and bad, through the happy and sad,
You have weathered, grown together, so well;
Through the sunshine and rain, through the peace and the pain,
All the love in your eyes clearly tell.

Such a blessing you have been to your family and friends,
Just to see how your marriage has endured;
The example you have set is never easy, and yet,
Many stars in your crown are assured!

TO GIL
(on our 44th anniversary)

If I had a magic wand and could give anything to you,
I would give you a week in Maine with Nubble Light in view.
We could walk the beach near the Cuttysark as often as we wished
Then find our way to Route 1A for a delicious dinner of fish.
We'd leave our worries all behind, just blue skies overhead;
Then watch the moon dance on the waves as we lie at night in bed.

But since I have no magic wand, I'll give you what I can--
A heart of love and helpfulness, for I'm your biggest fan.
I know your heart and am thankful for the years the Lord has blessed--
He's led us through the joys of life and brought us through many a test.
And now, here we are after all this time, with most of our lives behind us;
But our memories and the love we've shared are the glue in the ties that bind us!

LYDIA'S SEVENTEEN

Seventeen's so "in-between"--
Not sweet sixteen, nor yet eighteen;
No big to-do, a bit mundane—
Just marks a year has passed, again!
Yet seventeen's a time for dreams,
To think about what your life means;
A time to plan, to work, and pray
To honestly choose the better way!
And seventeen's a time for fun
With friends who'll dance a time in the sun;
A few might last, some you will forget,
But all will weave you in their net.
Through light and dark the year's your own,
May it be special—one in which you'll have grown.
In years to come, may you smilingly dream
Of the memories of having been seventeen!

LYDIA—UPON YOUR GRADUATION

Wherever you go, whatever you do,
Remember the Lord says: "I have plans just for you;
"To prosper, not harm you; to give you great hope,
"And through life's daily struggles, I'll help you to cope."
What more can you ask than this promise He makes
To be close beside every step that you take?
May your family and friends watch you reach for that star,
For it's what's in your heart that will help you go far!

Jer. 29:11

LYDIA JOY SESSIONS IS 18 TODAY

Lydia Joy Sessions is 18 today,
Poised on the brink of life coming your way;
With many new challenges and decisions ahead--
Your unwritten story, a book to be read.

We wish for you happiness and success and, yes, joy
In whatever endeavors you might choose to employ.
With God as your pilot we pray you'll be wise,
And through all your life you will reach for the skies!

MY DAUGHTER JAN

(Thought I'd recycle this poem written many years ago, but found I would not change a word)!

*My daughter Jan's a loving friend
Who senses more than most friends do;
She always lends a helping hand
And lifts my spirits when I'm blue.*

*Her happy smile, her cheerful way
Endears each one that she may meet;
But thoughtfulness, compassion, too,
Are traits that cause these friends to keep.*

*So blessed am I to have this one—
More than I am deserving of—
For no one has this gift from God
More than our Jan—the gift of love.*

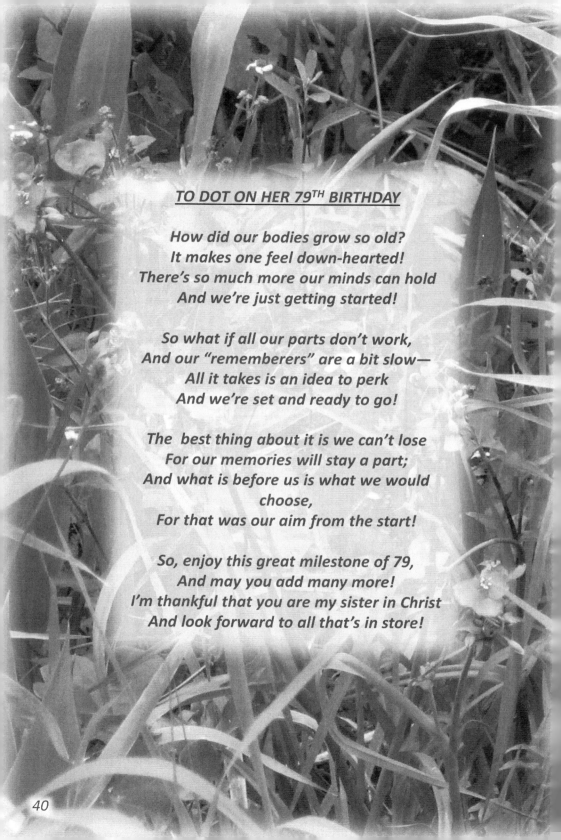

TO DOT ON HER 79TH BIRTHDAY

How did our bodies grow so old?
It makes one feel down-hearted!
There's so much more our minds can hold
And we're just getting started!

So what if all our parts don't work,
And our "rememberers" are a bit slow—
All it takes is an idea to perk
And we're set and ready to go!

The best thing about it is we can't lose
For our memories will stay a part;
And what is before us is what we would choose,
For that was our aim from the start!

So, enjoy this great milestone of 79,
And may you add many more!
I'm thankful that you are my sister in Christ
And look forward to all that's in store!

TO SHAWN

We hope your year is full of wins,
Not only when you play
But in the way you live your life—
In what you do and say.
You're really special to us all;
We're watching "from the stands"
With cheers for every "point you score"—
We're some of your greatest fans!

RYAN'S GRADUATION

Oh, young man Ryan,
you may blow your own horn!
Accept all those honors—
for this time you were born!
You have been blessed with
those talents you own—
May you keep on perfecting
your own "mellow tone!"
Whatever you're dreaming
we pray they'll come true;
You'll be hearing our "Bravos!"
And
CONGRATULATIONS TO YOU!

TO BRETT

To a classy young man with talents galore—
With your music and artwork and writings and more—
May this birthday be the beginning of many great things,
And may the delights of your heart soar on strong eagle wings.
We wish for success in whatever you do;
And above all our prayer's that the Lord will bless you!

TO GIL ON YOUR 87TH

So you've reached eighty-seven
One step closer to Heaven
(But not ready to knock at the door);
There are things left to do yet;
There are people you've not met,
And places to see just once more.

May each day be a blessing;
No need to be guessing
How many the Lord's planned for you.
No matter the day-amount,
It's your heart-beat that does count,
And He'll lead you all the way through.

So get on with the living
The taking and giving
That makes living your life so worthwhile.
Shun the pain and the sorrow
Watch the sun shine tomorrow
And brighten each day with a smile!

TO JAN

In all the years since you were born,
you've brought me so much joy—
A goodly child, a quick-turned mind,
and a heart full of compassion.
You've grown in all the loving ways
that mother's hope and dream,
And have matured to womanhood with
a special flair and fashion.
What more to add? a God-filled heart;
a love of friends and family;
With ways of helping others being
constantly your passion.
So, Happy Birthday, daughter, may this
be a celebration
Of all your life up to this point plus
future generations
Who will be taught and influenced by
your love and dedication!

How blessed we've been to be a part,
myself above any other,
That God allowed the chance to be your
friend as well as your mother.
(And may I take this time to add the
love and blessings of your dad).

TO JAY
(on his 21st birthday)

No one can know my pride, my son,
To see the man you are become!
The years slip by so silently;
The joys, the cares, are history.
Where have they gone, those golden years,
Predominant with smiles, not tears?
But all this time the growth has come
In body, mind and Christendom.
I gave you earthly life, it's true,
But God gave Spirit unto you;
And what you are inside and out
Is all your own without a doubt.
One score plus one, thou art a man,
If years it be the laws demand;
But, oh, my heart is gladdened fair
To see the little boy still there!

TO JAY ON HIS 50TH BIRTHDAY

They must have passed by while I
was in slumber!
Where have those years gone? Where
did they go?
Melted away like Florida snow!
And now here you are in a new phase
of life—
A new home, a new family and a
lovely new wife—
A new beginning! What will you do
With the years that the Lord has
allotted to you?
We pray you'll use wisely the time you
are given
And walk by The Way that will lead
you to Heaven.
You know that we love you and
couldn't want less
Than a great HAPPY BIRTHDAY
and to know you've been blessed!

TO MOTHER ON HER 76TH BIRTHDAY

We talk of the things on our minds every day,
But somehow or other we never do say
What's in our hearts.

The love that we feel hopefully shows through
In the way that we live, in the things that we do—
Just for starts.

But added to this is respect very deep—
The example you set is one hard to keep
In all ways.

Your place in our hearts can be giv'n to no other,
And all of your childen will honor you, Mother,
All our days.

TO OUR FAMILY
12/25/12

We live every day in our usual way
Not thinking how much we are blessed
By the love we all share
With a family who cares
And forgives when we don't make the test.

We are all so diverse, show our best and our worst,
Still God made us family complete.
In the course of our days
We all go separate ways,
But home is the place our hearts meet.

So we thank you, dear Lord, we can live in accord,
Knowing You make it all worth the while;
May these memories made,
Though they may dim or fade,
In our hearts always cause us to smile.
      --Grandma

VALENTINE

That I am loved there is no doubt,
I see it every day;
Perhaps not in so many words,
But in so many ways.
The little hidden things you do
That leave my time so free,
That I might do those things I like
Speak "words of love" to me.

That you are loved I hope you know
How much you've blessed my life;
That I am thankful every day
That we are man and wife.
Through all the years you've stood by me,
(It's been your longest race!)
But you've endured and be assured--
No one could ever take your place!

WHO IS SHE?

Who is she, this little girl of mine
Whose eyes fill up if I but raise my voice?
What do I know of what goes in inside
This little one, the one that is called Joyce?

Such tender love's bestowed on all her dolls,
The mother-instinct blooming there so sweet;
The pliant one, the quiet one, the fawn,
This eldest child, the one who's so petite.

But turn and take a look at when she plays—
Her brother and her sister are her pawns;
Imagination reigns and she's the queen,
The ruler of the world, even beyond!

What will she be, this little girl of mine
When she is grown? What life will be her choice?
Perhaps she'll have all of these traits combined,
This little girl, the one that is called Joyce!

MY MODEL "G"

You say you like my model "G"?
They made 'em strong to last!
They just don't make 'em like they did—
That kind is from the past!
He may not be the latest style
And parts be hard to find;
But through the years he's run so well,
He's paid for, and he's mine!

OUR MOTHER

We have a little mother
Who's only 5-feet-0.
But there is never anyplace
Her little legs can't go!
She's such a busy lady
From dawn 'til set of sun
For she makes a point to finish
Whatever she's begun.
She's always here to help us all
Whenever we have need,
And shows us that she loves each one
With kindly word and deed.
So, when you meet our mother,
You may think that she is small;
She may need stools to reach the shelves,
But in our book—she's tall!

Irene M. (Miller) Albert
1903 - 1989

A PRAYER FOR MY FATHER
(on his 75th birthday)

Dear Heavenly Father, I come to you today
Asking a special blessing on my father, if I may.
Seventy and five years he has lived upon this earth;
A strong, hard-working man—I'm sure you know his worth.
It's not for riches that I ask for him, although
You've blessed him well—I'm thankful this is so;
But I would ask for good health through the years;
A time in which much happiness appears;
A time to share the wisdom he has learned,
And to enjoy the fruits of what he's earned;
That he might live a long time yet to come,
And in the end that You might take him home.

Joseph H. Albert
1902 - 1992

AN OPEN VERSE TO MY FATHER

My father is a man both energetic and
industrious.
He is the kind of person who goes ahead
and does things without making any fuss;
Then keeps on doing nice things even
though sometimes he doesn't
even get a "thank you."
What can you say to a man like that?
What can you do?
Well, I've thought and thought about it
and have come up with the notion
That about all you can do with a man like
that is to give him love and devotion
And try to be the kind of person he'd be
as proud to say, "That's my daughter,"
As I am to say, "That's my father!"

Poems for Friends

A POEM FOR YOUR BIRTHDAY, ANNETTE

Everyone needs a friend like Annette!
She just seems to know when you need her, and yet
Puts no burden upon you, just sharing in prayer,
And cheering you on through the burdens you bear.

So what do we wish for this good friend, so dear?
Not only a special day but a wonderful year
In which she is blessed by our Lord up above!
Yes, Happy Birthday, Annette! We pray in His love.

ANNETTE—

Hey! Do you know what is coming the 5th day of May?
Can't think of much special-- it's just Saturday!
But maybe there's something that would make it stand out,
That we could remember and get excited about!
(Let me think...)

Oh! The on-coming weekend will bring one special day—
It's "Cinco de Mayo" as the Spanish would say;
"A time just to celebrate! No working today!"
"So it's 'hasta la vista'—we're going to play!"
(Good idea?!?)

Wow! There's something else happening that's coming your way;
For those "in the know," it's the "Big Derby Day!"
With horses and races and excitement galore—
Who could have planned it or wanted for more?!?
(Did you?)

But! All kidding aside, it is you we esteem,
And hope that your birthday is all that you dream!
We pray that our love will just wrap you around,
And God's blessings and peace through your year will abound!

HAPPY BIRTHDAY, STEVE!

We have a friend who lives "way down-Maine"
But he knows he is close to our hearts.
'Though we don't see this friend (seems like years without end,)
It's as though we've not long been apart!

Such a dear friend to name, one who's always the same,
One who listens and shares equal-time;
And His love of the Lord binds us in sweet accord—
A friend such as this is a "find!"

So we wish him a day and the year on the way
When God's blessings are heaped on his *head;
But we fear there will be (before eternity)
When his prayers aren't "amen-ed" but "ayuh-ed!"

*Southern pronunciation "hay-ud"

TO MARY—

She's small but she's mighty; she 6 years and 90,
A lady I met yesterday.
In her eyes was a smile and in just a short while
It seemed like I'd known her always.

She's sweet and she's caring; we had moments sharing
Our mutual love of The Lord--
Not in so many words, but the things that I heard
Said our hearts surely beat with accord.

I'm so glad that I met her, I'll not soon forget her;
Her blessing sure gladdened my heart.
On her special birthday, (let's call it her "worth-day");
"... above rubies..." sounds right from the start.

May the Lord bless you, Mary, do not be contrary
When His blessings are showered on you,
For we are believing that you are receiving
What you've given to others your life through!

FOREVER FRIENDS
(In memory of Margaret Quinn)

Way back in the time of "drill-team days"
When the distance between Leominster and Amesbury was still "quite-a-ways,"
Two young girls met and were instantly drawn
By the similarities of things of which they were fond,
For both would be fifteen within ten days of that meeting;
And thinking they might never see each other except when competing,
They decided to become "pen-pals."

Although over the years life had its twists and its turns,
They each knew the other could be trusted with her concerns—
A sounding-board, as it were, someone not so involved—
A new thought or perspective to help problem-solve.
'Mid their friendly reminders of the time flying by--
The changes the years wrought sometimes brought a sigh;
But they were content.

And that's how it began 66 years ago.
The letters and cards (with a few phone calls thrown in) had their ebb and flow;
But they each knew the other would always be there
To share laughter or heartache, affirming her care.
What a blessing such friendship has been through the years
As they wait for the place of no heartache and tears.
And that will be just the beginning.

ON TURNING 90...

The golden years have tarnished,
The fire has turned to ash,
And when the Lord comes calling
I'll be ready in a flash!
But 'til that time's upon me,
My smile will be in place;
With the love of fiends and family
I will surely win the race!

TO OUR FRIEND ON HIS 90TH BIRTHDAY

May you celebrate your years of life,
The happy and the sad;
The changes through the years you've seen
(Not all of them were bad);
The people you have loved and lost;
The places you have been;
The memories that come and go
Though you can't remember when.
This gift of life you have received—
With years you have been blest—
And may you treasure every day
With love and peace and rest!

TO ANN—

A very special lady,
One whom we admire;
And although she's reached "the age"
She probably won't retire!
Like the Energizer bunny,
She'll probably never stop,
And just keep on a-doin'
'Til she's just about ready to drop!
So, Happy Birthday, Lady!
May your energy never end;
And may this year bring all good things
To our very special friend!

TO KAREN

If you were looking for a friend of the very best kind,
What are the qualities you would have in mind?
One who would share your love of the Lord;
Who would value your friendship in sweet accord;
A person who's generous and willing to share
Her things and her counsel and even her care;
One you can trust with the hurts of your heart
And know they'll be prayed for right from the start;
One who can laugh at herself when she's wrong
And thrill at the notes of a bird's lovely song;
One who is loyal, kind-hearted and true—
That's the kind of a friend God's blessed me in you!

TO LUCILLE

What is your secret?
(You know you can tell!)
Would you let us all know
How you've lived long and well?
Is it all in your genes?
Do you not have a clue
Why the Lord chose to give
Many long years to you?

Think we all know the reason—
At least we can guess
That the Lord's chosen you
Many others to bless.
So we pray for good health
The coming year through,
And we send many wishes--
HAPPY BIRTHDAY TO YOU!

BETH—

It <u>seams</u> like you never get older!

No <u>thread</u> of evidence that you are;

But the date shows we <u>need(le)</u> to say

"HAPPY BIRTHDAY"

to the most original <u>pattern</u> by far!

In love and fun,

TO DECKER AND ANN

To say just what is felt is not an easy thing to do,
And just a simple "thanks" is quite inadequate, it's true;
For while you're praising others for the little things they've done,
You have been busy doing twice as much as anyone.
And though I do not thank you quite as often as I might,
You always have inspired me to do what's good and right.
I treasure most your friendship and the thoughtful things you do,
And in the quiet moments of my day, I thank God that I know you.

Special Occasions

A NURSE'S HANDS

Caring hands that tend to even the menial task;
Tender hands that help us all before we think to ask.
Comforting hands that soothe away much of our pain and fear;
Soft hands that gently wipe the wrinkled brow or baby's tear.
Loving hands that go beyond—how much we cannot tell;
Healing hands that put us on the road to being well.
Steady hands and calm resolve no matter where they're led, and
Praying hands for help to last through all the trials ahead.

A nurse's hands tell much about the one who serves this way,
Where God-given talent and great heart are needed every day.
We're thankful that you're there for us—we are your greatest fans—
And ask the Lord to bless you all, especially your nurse's hands.

TO DONNA
(Upon her retirement from Kroger)

We're not here to say farewell
But just to honor you with praise
As you have reached a point in life
Where you begin a brand new phase:
A time to rest, a time to read,
A time to take a long vacation;
To do those things you like to do
That make for calm and relaxation.

So many mem'ries, so many years,
Of loading carts and shelving stock;
Of friends who are like family,
And shoppers who just love to talk!
Yes, you will miss a whole lot more
(Including those important meetings);
But what we'll miss the most of all
Are your smiles and Wednesday morning greetings!

So take this time to start anew,
It's not a time for tears and sorrow;
But don't forget your Kroger friends
While you enjoy what comes tomorrow!

THE IDEAL TEACHER

Armed with some of <u>Judy's</u> knowledge and preparation like <u>Jan D.</u>,
And could persevere like <u>Laura</u>—what a teacher I would be!
If like <u>Marj</u> my self-control could grow, and like Helen be more kind;
And show <u>Mary</u>'s enthusiasm in trying to improve my mind;
And would grow to appreciate God's wonders more as <u>Dawn</u> has learned to do;
And could have the skill that <u>Marilyn</u> has and <u>Dot A</u>'s self-discipline, too;
If I could do the work that <u>Diane</u> does and be helpful like <u>Shirley C.</u>;
And on top of all these coveted traits, add <u>Nancy</u>'s humility;
And have some of <u>Pat's</u> alertness and more concern for souls like <u>June</u>;
Be more patient like <u>Joanne</u> is—not discouraged soon;
With trustworthiness like <u>Sharon</u> has to do all that is right;
Like <u>Peg</u> be more understanding and try with all my might;
With <u>Dot B.</u>'s imagination, and <u>Jan M.</u>' cheerful way;
Add <u>Carol</u>'s sense of humor to brighten up the day;
What could I add to make my life the very best I can?
Oh, yes, I know what I should add—the loving ways of <u>Ann</u>!
Yes, we learn from one another, but our goal should never dim:
We'll be more effective teachers as we grow to be more like <u>Him</u>!

TO OUR BIBLE SCHOOL TEACHERS

No greater task, no nobler deed
Than sowing of the Master's seed
In tender hearts.
No sweeter joy on earth compare
To watching grow the seedlings there
That love imparts.
No weariness, no selfishness
Nor carelessness must stop the quest
To nurture them,
But keep on keeping on until
They grow to take their place in life
As Christ-like men.
No easy task, no thoughtless deed
This sowing of the Master's seed
Was given you;
So we have gathered here this night
To thank you and with love requite

HONOR TO WHOM HONOR IS DUE!

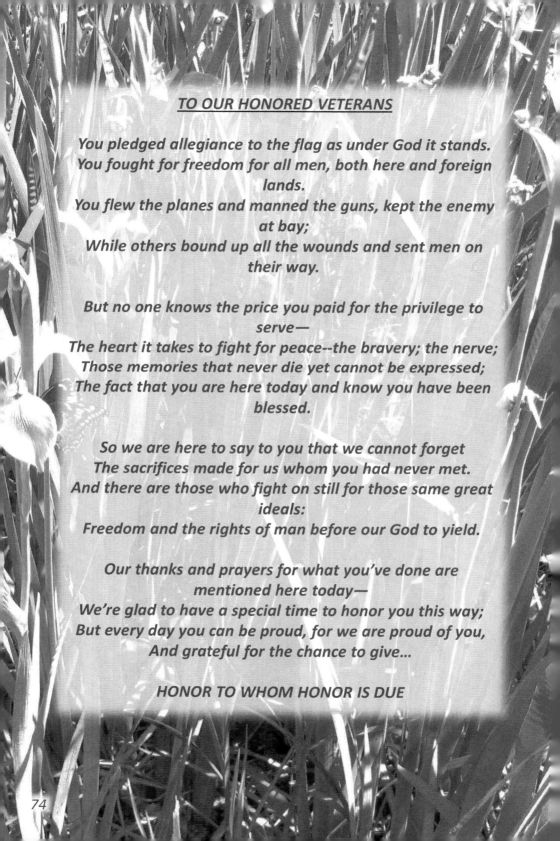

TO OUR HONORED VETERANS

You pledged allegiance to the flag as under God it stands.
You fought for freedom for all men, both here and foreign lands.
You flew the planes and manned the guns, kept the enemy at bay;
While others bound up all the wounds and sent men on their way.

But no one knows the price you paid for the privilege to serve—
The heart it takes to fight for peace--the bravery; the nerve;
Those memories that never die yet cannot be expressed;
The fact that you are here today and know you have been blessed.

So we are here to say to you that we cannot forget
The sacrifices made for us whom you had never met.
And there are those who fight on still for those same great ideals:
Freedom and the rights of man before our God to yield.

Our thanks and prayers for what you've done are mentioned here today—
We're glad to have a special time to honor you this way;
But every day you can be proud, for we are proud of you,
And grateful for the chance to give…

HONOR TO WHOM HONOR IS DUE

YOUR NURSE'S FEET

Blessed are the feet that run
To ease the pain of we who cry;
Who lie in bed and contemplate
The reason why.

Blessed are the feet that walk
So slowly with us down the hall;
A friend indeed to see us
Through it all.

Blessed are the feet that bring
Uplifting news of joy and hope;
Who try to keep our spirits up
And help us cope.

Blessed are your tired feet
That take you home when day is through,
Knowing when you leave this place
There's more to do.

Thank you for your blessed feet,
Those mercy-bringing feet of love;
Thanks also to our Heavenly Father
Up above.

Card Sentiments

A SPECIAL CARD

A special card for a special you
Complete with love and prayers, too;
For only God can ease your pain
And make you well and strong again.
Until that time, we'll cheer you on,
And welcome you back where you belong.

A YEAR OF BLESSINGS

May this year bring you blessings you've never foreseen—
The result of your work and your love;
May God guide you to places that you've never been
Reflecting His light from above.
Hope your day is made special by family and friends
As they offer best wishes to you,
For you've given us all the very best that you can
And we appreciate all that you do!

BIRTHDAY WISH

If I could have one wish for you, my special sister-friend,
It would be for a lightened heart to soar to Heaven's end
To see the wonders there for you that God has all prepared
As well as those right here that He has graciously shared.
So many things that cloud our days and block the sun of life;
So many things we'd like to change that only cause us strife;
But I am here to say to you that we can't change the world
Except the little part we're in (that scroll's not yet unfurled).
Believing God knows who you are and what you'd like to do,
I pray that all this coming year you'll see those dreams come true!

BEGINNING WITH A WONDERFUL BIRTHDAY!

GET WELL WISH

May your days be made brighter,
Your heart be made lighter,
And progress be made every day;
For you know that we care,
Asking God in our prayer,
That His comforts abide all the way.

MAY YOUR HEART KEEP ON SMILING

May your heart keep on smiling
in spite of the pain
Like the sun keeps on shining above
clouds and the rain.
May the Lord bless and keep you,
May He calm every cry;
While He comforts and heals you,
May you feel Him close by.

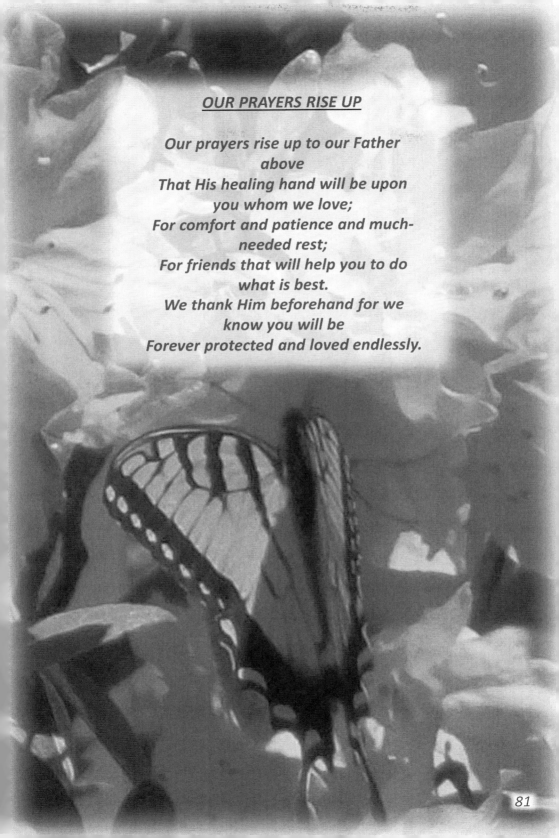

OUR PRAYERS RISE UP

Our prayers rise up to our Father above
That His healing hand will be upon you whom we love;
For comfort and patience and much-needed rest;
For friends that will help you to do what is best.
We thank Him beforehand for we know you will be
Forever protected and loved endlessly.

SEASON'S GREETINGS

*The weeks and months just seem to go by
faster every year,
And often we don't take the time for
those we hold most dear.
At times we think of each of you and
plan to call "today,"
But then the hours go sailing by
and "life" gets in the way!
And so we send a prayer of thanks
for you (we are confessing);
Although we may neglect to call,
you're among our greatest blessings!*

*Hope you have a wonderful holiday season
and a happy and blessed New Year!*

TO GIL S.

Some people get old before their time.
Some act too young, and that's just fine;
But those who mature gracefully
Who are yet young at heart
Make such good friends;
And that's just a start
Of all the nice things we'd like to say,
But they're all included in the words:
HAPPY BIRTHDAY!

MAY YOUR SHIP BE SAILING

May your ship be sailing into port;
May a special dream come true;
May this coming year bring peace of mind—
That's our birthday wish for you.

SYMPATHY FOR AN OLD CLASSMATE

*It has been many years since last we met.
You probably would not recognize me,
and yet
My heart goes out to you in your time
of grief.
I pray that time and tears will bring you
some relief;
For naught can fill the place your
loved one's left,
And even happy memories can leave
your heart bereft.
So if you find you can't explain to
any man,
Take it to God—for He will always
understand.*

TO RHEA

How blest you've been to share this time
with Walt through the years;
But now it's time to say good-bye with
smiling through your tears.

So bittersweet the partings come, for
you are tied to earth.
While Walt now knows the value of
what life for Him is worth.

So live to full what time is left,
for God has plans for you;
And he'll be there to greet you
when your time on earth is through.

UPON THE DEATH OF A CHRISTIAN

How softly the soul lifts from earth
up to Heaven!
We grieve at the passing with tears
gently flowing;
Assured that the Father is patiently
waiting,
We sweetly rejoice in our hearts
with the knowing.

THE RUDDER MAY BE DRAGGIN'

The rudder may be draggin'
And the wheels a little soft
But the Lord provides the power
And is keeping you aloft.

WHATEVER YOU WISH

Whatever you wish,
Whatever you dream,
May this be a great year for you;
So just be prepared,
And the blessings will come,
For the Lord will be seeing you through!

WITH THOUGHTS OF LOVE

Thinking of you with thoughts of love
And sending our prayers to the Father above;
That He will look down with compassion and care;
That you will look up, feel His presence is there.

WITH SYMPATHY

No one knows another's pain
Nor feels his sense of loss—
That emptiness that fills the soul
Can't be restored at any cost.
We pray that God who knows so well
May hold you close today;
Will ease your sorrow with His love
and wipe your tears away.

YOU'RE IN MY PRAYERS

You were in my prayers today.
I didn't know just what to say;
But Father knows just what you need,
Assured me you'd be blessed indeed.
He knows what you've been going through;
Will give you strength and courage, too.
He sees and comforts when you cry
And lets you know that He's close by.
So in His hands I'll leave you there
'Til we meet again in tomorrow's prayer.

YOUR BIRTHDAY IS A SPECIAL DAY

Your birthday is a special day,
The first day of your year;
A time for looking back to see
Events that brought you here,
The people who have touched your life,
The places you have seen,
Accomplishments that were your goals,
And some that "might-have-been."
But now it's time to look ahead
For what God has for you,
No matter where the course may lead
You know He'll see you through.
So celebrate the life you have,
Enjoy what you can give;
And let God's blessings cover you
While you sing and smile and live!

MAY YOUR SHIP BE SAILING INTO PORT

May your ship be sailing into port
With blessings in the hold,
Like love and peace and happiness
And shelter from the cold.
And may the Captain of your ship
Bring healing to you, too,
For we would want the very best
In our birthday wish for you!

JUST FOR YOU A PRAYER

Just for you a prayer
That wherever you are today,
The Lord will meet you there;
With comfort and peace and healing
And that calm-in-your-soul feeling
That transcends every heartache and care.

WHEN LIFE SEEMS HARD

We all have times when life seems hard
With pain we cannot share;
For there are things we must endure,
And no one seems to care.
But we are here to let you know
Our thoughts are with you there,
And hope you are encouraged by
Our lifting your name in prayer.

A PRAYER FOR HEALING

As springtime follows winter,
And sunshine follows rain,
May healing and good health
    be yours
And pain-free once again.

WHEN THINKING OVER LIFE

When thinking over life's great gifts
And what has meant the most,
We think of those who've shown God's love—
To you we raise a toast.
"To special friends and family
With whom we have been blessed:
We wish you joy and peace and health.
And all His very best!"

Whimsical

TODAY I AM EIGHTY

Today I am eighty,
A veritable old lady
Who most days feels younger by far!
I run every day
(The washing machine, by the way)
And hike 50 feet to the car!

So you see I am well
And ready to tell
How the Golden Years don't bother me!
There's nothing to dread—
It's all in your head.
*Now what did I do with my coffee?!?

*Last line kibbitzed by daughter Joyce

TO JAN UPON LOSING HER TOOTH

The magic fairy came to town
And she went looking all around
For precious little white ivory bones
That fairies use as jewelry stones.

        She came at night
        When the moon was right
        To find a child
        And make him smile;
        And if a tooth's place
        Had an empty space,
        She'd make a wish
        And start to fish
        Under the pillow
        With her wand of willow;
        And then, forsooth,
        With the precious tooth,
        She'd fly away
        Before break of day!

But so the little child wouldn't cry,
Some shiny new silver she'd place nearby.
And when the child woke in the morn,
He'd find some money but his tooth would be gone!

So, one of these days if you look very hard,
You might see a fairy dance out in the yard;
And she could be wearing your tooth with her bells
In her necklace or bracelet—you never can tell!

KITTIE'S LATE-NIGHT ESCAPADE

Kittie sits beside me on the bed
And purrs. If she could talk instead
She might be saying thanks for my small share
In saving her from the clutches of a pair
Of many dogs who have us on their roam
Of midnight prowls. They chased her home
Right onto the porch! No noise she made
But then I heard a thump and was afraid;
Jumped from my bed expecting robbers there,
And, peeking out, I saw that critter-pair.
I noisily unlocked the sunporch door
And stepped out. All was quiet as before;
But Kittie, hackles up, was on the sill,
The curtain down. She looked a little ill.
We came into the house, the trouble o'er,
Hoping to get to sleeping as before;
But, lo, our little escapade had woke
My husband. Not a word he spoke
But took his robe and slippers to the den
For a little peace and quietude. So then—
Kittie sits beside me on the bed
And purrs. One-thirty-six the clock just read.
Here we are together, her and me,
Wide awake, my husband missing, angrily.
"Thanks a lot, Kittie!" I snidely say to her;
But she just rubs my arm, looks up at me and
purrs!

What a blessing it's been to see my work in this book!
I'm finding poems everywhere since beginning to look;
So if you don't see <u>your</u> verse, it's hiding somewhere
In a drawer or notebook or my brain, waiting there!

I hope you enjoyed what is here on these pages;
You probably guessed they were written in stages—
From the time Jan was little and lost her first tooth
To this missal today when I'm "Just Older Youth!"

I want you to know you are welcome to use
Whatever you find here that will bless or amuse.
Just sign on my name, we'll be friends from the start,
For what I'm sharing with you is all from my heart!

Marge

P.S. Would love to know where my poems have gone –
    You can contact me at gmargil3@juno.com! ☺

Made in the USA
San Bernardino, CA
22 April 2014